Empath

The Complete Survival Guide For The Empath: The Ultimate Guide For Sensitive People - Understand & Embrace Your Gift, & Use This Energy To Thrive!

Jane Aniston

Table of Contents

Introduction

Chapter 1: What is an Empath?
What's So Bad About Being an Empath?

Chapter 2: Problems the Empath May Encounter
Social Anxiety

Depression

Anxiety

Intimacy

Seeing Too Much

Chapter 3: Defending Yourself as an Empath
Setting Energetic Boundaries

How to Set Boundaries

You Need to Be Happy to Make Others Happy

Ground Yourself

Using Crystals to Protect Yourself

Visualization Technique

Chapter 4: Learn to Control Your Abilities

Meditation

The Scan and the Check

Create a Personal Mantra

To Block or Not to Block, That is the Question

Taking Good Care of Yourself

Essential Tips to Stay Healthy

Recharging Strategies

Get Enough Sleep

Bathing

Smoothies

Journaling

Practical Exercises

Making Use of Affirmations

Being Assertive

Reducing Negativity

Chapter 5: Managing Your Own Emotions

Dealing With Repressed Feelings

Acknowledge

Choose to Stay

Examine

Accept

Set Your Intentions

Breathe

Releasing Negative Emotions

Using Crowded Area to Your Advantage

Enlist the Help of Audio

Chapter 6: Keep Yourself Clear of Psychic Baggage

Returning Energy

Psychic Attacks and Energy Vampires

Why are These People Like This?

Energetic Cording

Cutting the Cord

Conclusion

A message from the author

Introduction

The simple fact that you picked up this book leads me to believe that either you, or someone that you care about, is an empath. It doesn't matter which of these is true, this book has been written to allow you a fascinating insight into the world of the empath.

Empaths are highly sensitive to the emotions of others and this sensitivity can be misinterpreted by those who do not understand it. Empaths often feel as though they are the odd ones out and battle to keep a handle on their emotions.

In this book, we will look at how to deal with your emotions, common problems that an empath may have, protecting yourself as an empath and clearing yourself of psychic baggage.

Perhaps you, as an empath, have long wanted to free yourself of this "curse". This book is not going to help you with that. What this book is going to do, however, is to teach you to see your ability for what it really is, a gift.

Once you are able to appreciate that you have a gift, it becomes a lot easier to learn how to use it to your advantage. And this book is going to help you to do all that and more.

You will learn useful tools to help prevent you from feeling overwhelmed and start thoroughly enjoying having your gift.

You will learn how to use your unique gift to improve your life and the lives of those around you.

Are you ready? Let's get started.

© **Copyright 2017 by Eddington Publishing - All rights reserved.**

This document is geared towards providing exact and reliable information in regards to the topic and issue covered. The publication is sold with the idea that the publisher is not required to render accounting, officially permitted, or otherwise, qualified services. If advice is necessary, legal or professional, a practiced individual in the profession should be ordered.

- From a Declaration of Principles which was accepted and approved equally by a Committee of the American Bar Association and a Committee of Publishers and Associations.

In no way is it legal to reproduce, duplicate, or transmit any part of this document in either electronic means or in printed format. Recording of this publication is strictly prohibited and any storage of this document is not allowed unless with written permission from the publisher. All rights reserved.

The information provided herein is stated to be truthful and consistent, in that any liability, in terms of inattention or otherwise, by any usage or abuse of any policies, processes, or directions contained within is the solitary and utter responsibility of the recipient reader. Under no circumstances will any legal responsibility or blame be held against the publisher for any reparation, damages, or monetary loss due to the information herein, either directly or indirectly.

Respective authors own all copyrights not held by the publisher.

The information herein is offered for informational purposes solely, and is universal as so. The presentation of the information is without contract or any type of guarantee assurance.

The trademarks that are used without any consent, and the publication of the trademark is without permission or backing by the trademark owner. All trademarks and brands within this book are for clarifying purposes only and are the owned by the owners themselves, not affiliated with this document.

Chapter 1

What is an Empath?

Almost every person alive is empathic to some degree. It is part of what makes us, us. It helps us relate better to others and to understand them. Empathy is, essentially, being able to identify with other people.

The level of empathy experienced differs from person to person. Some people, like sociopaths, have little or no empathy at all. For "normal" people, empathy helps them to move through their world – they feel empathetic in the moment but the feelings wear off when they are out of that situation.

Empaths, on the other hand, can be said to feel too much. This is not always a bad thing but it can become very tiring. Empaths will over-identify with those they connect with because they are able to pick up on their energy and emotion.

This, in turn, can lead to them feeling drained, confused and overwhelmed.

At a very basic level, the world is made up of energy. Each form of this energy has its own vibrational frequencies. Empaths are more easily able to pick up on this energy – whether in humans, animals or places and things.

An empath will often be able to tell what is to be discussed before the words are uttered. But it goes beyond this – they are able to read subtle cues in body language, movements, tone of voice, etc.

When they put all of this information together, they are great at communicating. In some cases, this registers as a sort of precognition.

An empath will often pick up on unseen energies in a given situation or place. They might, for example, go into a room where a couple has just had an argument and might be able to sense that negative vibes in the room.

And this will often happen unconsciously. They might not actively be looking for any particular vibes but their unconscious mind will still be working at finding vibes.

Most empaths can also be described as highly creative and capable of exuding great charm.

What's So Bad About Being an Empath?

If you are not an empath yourself, and have read what I have just written about this, you will probably be wondering why anyone would hate being an empath themselves. The truth is that these "abilities" can be quite useful but they can also cause problems. Unless you are an empath, this is something that you just cannot understand.

Empaths, by nature of their gift, are able to absorb the energies of those around them, whether they want to or not. This results in them feeling exactly what those around them feel.

Now, when the other people are happy, everything is fine. When things go the other way, though, this can be overwhelming for the empath.

Many empaths become imprinted with the emotions, etc. experienced by those around them and become less able to identify what it is that they personally want and feel.

They will very often ignore their own issues because they feel the pain that others are experiencing. People who need help are naturally drawn to empaths and this can make things hard for the empath in general.

Imagine, if you will, going to the ice cream store and buying forced to eat every single flavor of ice cream, whether you like it or not. Initially, the experience is bound to be interesting and maybe even fun.

Eventually, however, you are going to want to stop. You will have had enough of the ice cream and feel overwhelmed by it.

The same can be said of an empath —except that they are dealing with feelings and not ice cream.

Those who speak to an empath will usually come away with a feeling of relief, even if it is only because they feel that the empath understands them. People do tend to seek out the empath for help during troubled times and the empath ends up having to deal with a lot of negativity.

Chapter 2

Problems the Empath May Encounter

In this chapter, we will have a look at problems that the empath might encounter.

Social Anxiety

Being anxious is not a nice thing. It saps the energy from us – energy that could be better spent elsewhere.

For most empaths, social anxiety is something that they need to deal with. A study published in 2011 found that a correlation between hypersensitivity to other people's thoughts and the possibility of having a social phobia.

The study found that participants, despite being highly anxious, were accurate when it came to what they perceived to be the feelings of those they interacted with.

Where this can become a problem is when the other person's negative feelings or distress are also keenly felt. The brain, in an effort to protect itself from these negative feelings, tended to create feelings of anxiety in order to protect itself. Those who had developed social anxiety were believed to have done so as a protection mechanism.

It is common for empaths to be more introverted in nature, and to want to isolate themselves.

Depression

It is not uncommon for an empath to feel depressed. It can result from a feeling of being different or misunderstood or it can be as a result of feeling overwhelmed.

Depression can also act as a real defense for the empath as it dampens their abilities.

Anxiety

There is a great deal of subtle energy and sensory input in the environment and this can overstimulate the empath. When it becomes too much to handle, they end up feeling anxious and unable to cope.

They might look at those around them and see that they are coping. This leads to greater feelings of inadequacy and anxiety.

The problem here is that the empath works on the false assumption that everyone else is going through the same kind of turmoil that they are, but are coping with it far better.

They tend to feel anxious about the present and what will happen in the future. There is a general feeling of dread – that something bad could happen at any given moment.

This anxiety makes it difficult to enjoy life and to live it to the full.

What the empath needs to realize, however, is that everyone else also has problems. The anxiety that the empath is feeling is a good indicator of that – they are picking up the signals from others.

When they come to terms with the fact that their own anxious feelings are being intensified by the feelings of those around them, they can start working through them properly and stop feeling so alone.

Intimacy

For an empath, developing a truly intimate relationship can be an extremely challenging task. It means allowing someone to get close enough to them to share those parts of themselves that they don't usually let anyone else see.

It means dropping all defenses and trusting that things will go well.

For most empaths, it is this dropping of defenses that proves to be the most difficult challenge. It is easier to hide behind a façade than to really put themselves out there.

They worry, at their core, that they will be exposed as inadequate or as abnormal.

In addition, the intimacy that results from being with a partner can be very trying for the empath. If they move in with their partner, they will have to deal with them every day and this can be exhausting for the empath.

For this reason, it is not unusual for an empath to stay single. In fact, they relish being alone because it gives them a break from the emotions of others. Over time, they no longer even need interaction with other people – they can become accustomed to being on their own and not being lonely.

Overcoming this is difficult but it can be done. For starters, the empath needs to realize that it is possible to have a healthy relationship in which both partners respect each other's boundaries.

Allowing themselves to be vulnerable is an important step for an empath – they must work towards the goal of being able to share everything that they are with their partner. Even if the relationship does not work out, the empath must be willing to take the chance, secure in the knowledge that they will be able to deal with any fallout.

At the heart of any healthy intimate relationship, is the love of who you are as a person. You need to be able to accept your faults and fears. Once that is accomplished, caring for others comes a whole lot more naturally.

Seeing Too Much

Being an empath means that you see a lot more than what the average person does. This can be troublesome in those instances where you see things that they would rather you had not. In these instances, the person may take steps to physically distance themselves from you.

It can be disheartening, but look at it from their point of view – imagine if you were around someone who knew that you were feeling insecure, even though they were trying to project an air of confidence. Someone that they could never really fool.

Now, it isn't that people are generally dishonest, but rather that they do want to be able to keep some of their own emotions and feelings hidden. As a result, they might find it easier to move away from the empath.

Chapter 3

Defending Yourself as an Empath

If you are not an empath, it is difficult to understand exactly what the empath goes through on a day to day basis. If you are an empath and are trying to get someone to understand what it is like, the following exercise might help:

Walk into your home and switch on all the TV's, radios, alarm clocks, etc. If it can play a tune, turn it on. Turn the volume to high and just take in all the noise. Concentrate on each and every song/ tone that is playing.

How long did you last? Was it hard to keep track of what was happening and when it was happening? I'll bet it was. Did you start to feel overwhelmed? Of course you did. Did you want it all to stop? Most certainly.

Well, you now have an idea of what it is like for an empath when they are constantly surrounded by people. Except that the background noise that they experience is in the form of feelings.

The empath needs to protect themselves or they will end up being overwhelmed all the time. In this chapter, we will go through how to tune out that background "noise".

Setting Energetic Boundaries

It is important for the empath to learn how to hold on to their positive energy and shield themselves from absorbing too much negative energy from others.

To do this, the empath must develop defined, strong boundaries.

How to Set Boundaries

For the empath, the struggle is that they are so in tune with what other people are wanting or feeling that they end up not having the ability to feel their own in-depth needs.

With the empath being so affected by negative energy, it is doubly important to establish firm boundaries so that they are able to protect their own energy levels. Whenever they are dealing with others, they need to ensure that they stick to their boundaries firmly.

The first step is to realize a very simple truth – it is not the empath's job to make everyone else happy. This is something that goes against the very grain of the empath's makeup but it is something that they need to fully embrace if they want to get as much out of life as possible.

You Need to Be Happy to Make Others Happy

If you are miserable, you are not much good to anyone. While you might be able to complete tasks assigned to you, you will burn out a lot more quickly if you are doing things that you don't really want to do.

As an empath, you need to work on your self-confidence and start to realize that you do not have to do everything people ask you to in order to get them to like you. It's natural to want to be liked and so it is also natural to always want to put other's needs ahead of your own.

If you do that consistently though, you are setting yourself up for failure. For starters, you are giving yourself the message that what you want is of little to no importance and this is no good for your self-confidence.

Secondly, you are telling those around you that what you want is less important than what they want and so they will start to see things that way themselves.

What happens is that you end up agreeing to do things that make you unhappy and get to a point where you are burnt out. When you finally say, "No" because you can't take it anymore, the other person feels let down.

If, on the other hand, you only agree to do things when you feel up to it, you are less likely to burn yourself out and will have more energy overall.

Start today by building up your own self-confidence. Save some time every day to do something that makes you feel good and that you can look forward to.

When someone asks you to do something, actually consider whether you truly want to do it or not. If you do not, simply say, "No" politely. You don't need to come up with a great excuse either. Most people will understand that you cannot always do what they ask and you shouldn't need to explain yourself.

Ground Yourself

Grounding yourself is about connecting to the Earth's energy. Being grounded allows you to draw on this energy and stability as and when you need it.

Here are ways that you can ground yourself:

- **Incense or Essential Oils:** Smudging your home with sage sticks, or burning cedar or sandalwood incense is an ancient trick for clearing the negative energy from your space.

- **Water:** When you truly feel in need of grounding, there is little better than immersing yourself in water. Water is neutral and can help to clear negative energy. It helps to drown out the background noise and ground you in a tangible way. Take a few seconds to relax and feel the negativity draining away from you and into the water.

- **Making Direct Contact with the Earth:** The simplest way to feel grounded is to take off your shoes and walk barefoot on the ground. Take a few seconds to relax and feel the energy flowing up into you from the earth. Feel yourself getting stronger and stronger.

Using Crystals to Protect Yourself

I like to think of crystals as Mother Nature's own battery packs. Each different crystal has its own particular energy and unique qualities. Crystals, when chosen carefully, will resonate with their users and help them to balance their own subtle energies.

Crystals provide gentle and effective spiritual protection and are particularly valuable to empaths. Whether you choose to incorporate crystals as jewelry or use them in their natural form, crystals can help you in your spiritual journey and protect you along the way.

In order to choose the right crystal for you, it is a good idea to go to a shop that sells a range of crystals and see if any stand out for you. You can then find out if the properties of that particular stone match what you are looking for. Nine times out of ten, they will – you will instinctively be drawn to the stone that has the same type of energy that you need.

Don't get too caught up in the individual properties of the stone – that is not as important as the resonance that you have with a particular stone. Most crystals will have protective properties and all can act as personal talismans.

As long as you choose a crystal that you are really drawn to, you are bound to make the right choice.

Crystals that are great for protection include rose quartz, lapis lazuli, carnelian, tiger's eye and tourmaline.

Visualization Technique

Start by finding a peaceful spot where you will not be disturbed. Take a moment to breathe in and out very deeply and disconnect from your worries. Repeat this a few times. The objective here is to become calm and relaxed.

When your mind feels calmer, focus your attention on your breathing. Take a deep breath in and feel the air fill your lungs and stretch your diaphragm. Hold the breath to the count of four.

Breathe out slowly, this time visualizing the breath coming out in the form of an energy bubble. As you breathe out, the bubble gets bigger and bigger until it completely envelopes your body.

Visualize the bubble extending out past your fingertips and creating a layer of protection against the outside world.

Once your bubble is big enough, you can start breathing normally again.

You can repeat this exercise every day or before a particularly trying situation. You can change the size of the bubble to suit your particular circumstances. For example, if you feel that you want to be smaller and less noticeable, you can contract the bubble so that it hugs your body more.

If you want, on the other hand, to be more noticeable, like when you have to give a speech, for example, you can make the bubble larger.

Visualize your bubble as being a protective energy layer around you – energy cannot gain admittance to this bubble at all. So, even if someone is standing really close to you, you cannot be affected by their energy.

You can take this one step further by visualizing the bubble pushing away negative energy.

By doing this, you are taking personal responsibility for protecting your aura. Most people are unaware that they need to do this and so end up soaking up negative energy that they do not need to.

By creating this bubble, you not only protect yourself from the negative energy of others but you also prevent them from being able to drain your energy as well.

This visualization exercise will get easier with time. If you consistently practice this exercise, you will reach a point when this becomes an automatic process, allowing you to control what energy comes in or leaves without giving it much thought at all.

Think of it as you would a schoolyard. You put a fence around the outside of the schoolyard to prevent the school kids wandering off and to prevent undesirable elements coming in.

Our energy is a lot like the school children in the above image – if you don't make any effort to control it, it will become unfocused and you will lose a lot of it.

By following the bubble visualization, however, you are creating a space for the aura to reside in, you are giving it set boundaries. You are also helping to reduce the chance of people taking the energy or it simply dissipating.

Chapter 4

Learn to Control Your Abilities

Don't you wish there was some kind of switch that allowed you to turn your empath abilities on or off at will? Unfortunately, it's nothing quite as simple as that. That does not mean, however, that you have no control whatsoever.

Through the exercises in this chapter, you will start to learn how to better control your gift.

Meditation

For an empath, meditation is the key to creating an inner feeling of serenity and a more contented existence. Meditation helps to reset both your body and mind. You can incorporate visualization into your meditation to make it even more effective in the long term.

Try imagining yourself enveloped by a bundle of clear, protective and loving energy. Watch as negativity bounces off this protective layer, completely unable to penetrate it.

The Scan and the Check

You can do this during a meditation or at any stage of the day when you have time. Do this before you even set foot out of your door so that you can be better prepared for what you may encounter.

Scanning your body in your mind helps you to notice what pains or emotions are being held within your body/ mind. That will help you when you come into contact with issues that other people have – you will know what emotions belong to you and what emotions belong to them.

Create a Personal Mantra

Creating a personal protection mantra will be useful for those situations where you need help but it is not possible to either ground yourself or to meditate. It does not have to be anything too elaborate. Something as simple as, "I am protected and loved" can work very well.

The trick is to choose a mantra that you believe is true. So, if you use the mantra in the example above, it is not enough to say, "I am protected and loved", you also have to believe that you are.

You can repeat this in your mind several times a day and especially when you feel in need of protection. Repeat it while you are doing your visualizations with the bubble or the light to reinforce them even more.

To Block or Not to Block, that is the Question

As you progress along your journey, you will start to learn how to block out any energy that comes from the outside. It can become almost automatic. It may even seem the safest way to live.

But, is it really living? Yes, you are safeguarded against any negative energy but you are also missing out on potentially positive energy as well.

To truly live, you need to understand what is going on around you and take part in the experience. This means that your boundary needs to become a little more flexible. Instead of visualizing a bubble or light that blocks out any form of energy, you can choose something that does allow positive energy in.

There is a caveat here though, when you start out, it is best to block any external energy. When you become more adept at using your own powers, you can start allowing positive energy in again.

Taking Good Care of Yourself

Everyone needs to take good care of themselves in order to be able to live the fullest life possible. This is especially true of the empath. You need to eat nutritious food in order to prevent yourself from getting burned out.

You also need to keep your body active and give yourself plenty of downtime during which you can be alone. For "normal" people, this may seem as though you are shutting yourself away in order to avoid the outside world. What they don't understand, however, is that an empath requires solitude to thrive.

If you are not able to get as much alone time as you would like, the next best thing is to concentrate on keeping yourself as healthy as possible.

Essential Tips to Stay Healthy

You need to choose a diet that is rich in natural nutrients and whole, good foods. A simple approach here is to steer clear of foods that have more than 3-5 ingredients in them or that contain ingredients that you cannot pronounce. Just by doing this, you will cut out a lot of unhealthy food from the get-go.

Sugar is not your friend and neither are stimulants. Your system is already highly keyed, revving it up more will just cause you to experience burnout faster. Scrap that morning coffee and steer clear of highly processed, refined carbs.

Exercise every day to help alleviate stress and get rid of negative feelings that you may have soaked up. You don't have to spend four hours a day in the gym. Just aim for about half an hour of physical activity a day, in total. What exercise you do makes no difference – as long as it raises your heartrate. You can even split up the exercise into smaller sessions to get it done.

Take a forest bath. This is something that originated in Japan and that can be extremely useful at restoring you to health. The basic idea is to spend some time out in nature, preferably in amongst trees. Not only does this get you out into the fresh air, but it also means communing with the natural world. It is believed that trees exude healing energies so do take some time out of your day to get back to nature.

Get some sunshine. Working in an office is all very good and well but you do also need daily exposure to the sun for radiant good health. Get out into the sun for at least 15-20 minutes a day so that your body is able to produce Vitamin D.

Recharging Strategies

Next, we need to consider some basic strategies that will help you to keep your energy clean and radiant for the better part of the day. If you spend some time working on these exercises, you will find that your health improves and you start to feel better automatically.

If you want to create the maximum positive effect, you need to ensure that you recharge and clear your energy on a regular basis.

Get Enough Sleep

Being adequately rested is one of the most important things in keeping an empath healthy. If you are sleep deprived, you cannot function as effectively as you should and you will be less able to fend off negative energy or prevent your own energy being drained.

Unfortunately for most empaths, sleep disturbances are relatively common. This could be as a result of the emotions that they have to deal with on a daily basis or just because they are a lot more sensitive to external noise and light.

For most empaths, the first step to sleeping soundly is to have the room pitch dark. This means installing heavy curtains and black out blinds so that no light can enter the room. This also means ensuring that all electronic appliances within the room that have some kind of LED display are banished or switched off.

That means switching the TV off at the plug so that the standby light goes off and ditching the LED bedside alarm clock.

Even with all this in place, the room may not be dark enough. An empath should consider wearing a sleeping mask to block out further light. Choose one in a natural material like cotton so that your skin can breathe while you are wearing it.

Once the light has been taken care off, it is time to clear out as much sound as possible. This means removing appliances that may make a noise and possibly sleeping on your own instead of with your partner.

It also helps to get a pair of earplugs. A set of soft silicon plugs are useful in this as they fit into the ear well and can be safely washed. You will need to replace the plugs periodically.

It is also a good idea to switch off your electronics at least an hour before bed time. Make it a rule to switch off your TV, phone, etc. at the cut-off time at night so that your body knows it is sleep time.

Bathing

Bathing is extremely soothing and can help to cut stress short for you. Add a cup of sea salt and a cup of Epsom salts to your bath. (Skip this if you have high blood pressure.) Soak in the bath to relax and repair tired muscles and cleanse your aura. You need to be submerged in the water from your toes to your neck for at least twenty minutes.

Smoothies

Smoothies can be a shortcut for good health and a way to incorporate healthier foods in a more palatable manner. Let's say, for example, you cannot stand the taste of carrots. When you whizz them up in a blender with natural yoghurt, a handful of berries and a banana, this won't matter because you won't even taste them. Smoothies are quick and easy to prepare with no cooking required.

Journaling

In order to be healthy and happy as an empath, you need to have a deep understanding of the way you think and what does and does not work for you. This entails understanding how certain situations impact you, how the food you eat impact you, etc.

Keeping a journal can be an extremely useful exercise in identifying problem areas and trigger situations that need to be avoided.

Practical Exercises

There is always going to be some temptation to shut yourself off from those around you when you are an empath. There are going to be times that you feel as though you are not able to handle the emotions that are put out.

The problem with this is that you can become quite accustomed to your isolation and lose touch with the outside world even more. It is important to maintain some form of social contact to prevent that from happening.

For some empaths, distracting themselves becomes their chosen coping mechanism. Distracting yourself can be helpful but it is not always good for you. Getting drunk or high is a form of distraction, as is jumping into bed with a stranger or overindulging in junk food. None of these, however, are healthy.

Whilst they do act as a means of distraction, they also change the subtle energies in our body and shift them to a more negative space. Pigging out on that cheeseburger may make you feel better for now, but it will have a negative impact if done on a regular basis.

In this chapter, you will be taught distractions that are healthy and helpful to you.

Making Use of Affirmations

Most of us have heard of affirmations. They are a lot like the personal mantra you came up with earlier. They are positive statements that you repeat a number of times every day, the idea being that the more they are repeated, the more your subconscious will start to believe them.

Much like the personal mantra, it is imperative that you believe the affirmations that you are using. It is for this reason that it is a good idea to come up with one that means something to you.

You could, for example, say something like, "Life is good, love comes easily."

The main thing is that the affirmation is positive and that it is believable. You should not use negative language in your affirmation. So, saying something like, "Bad things won't happen" is not a good affirmation because it is negative and also very unlikely – bad things happen to everyone.

On the other hand, "Good things happen to me all the time" is a good example because it is positive and can also be true.

Being Assertive

It might seem unusual for this to follow a discussion about distractions, but think about it for a second. Do you always want to say "Yes" when someone asks you something? Most empaths do. But isn't this just another form of distraction?

You don't want to deal with potential conflict so you say, "Yes".

Here's another way to deal with the situation – let's say that someone asks you to go to a movie with them.

Instead of flatly saying, "No", you could tell them that you need to check your calendar and that you'll call them later.

This is a way of dealing with the situation that is conflict-free and that also allows you to really consider whether or not you want to go to the movie. You are being assertive here.

Assertiveness is not something that always comes naturally to the empath. But assertiveness is important to your own self-esteem. You also have the right to want things to go your way, and to do things in a manner that supports your own aspirations.

Here are some sentences for you to finish. Working through this exercise will help you to restyle your life along lines healthier for you and help you to lead a more contented life:

I have the right to ask for …

What is it that you need? Do you need some space? More consideration?

It is alright to … in order to maintain my energy level so I can function optimally.

What do you want to say no to? What would you rather do?

If I say, "No", the other person might …

They may be disappointed, they may be annoyed, etc. The chances are that it won't be as much of a big deal as you might have built it up to be in your mind.

If you do not show enough respect for yourself to thoroughly consider your own needs when you are creating boundaries, how do you expect others to? By always doing what someone else wants you to, you are effectively telling them and yourself that their needs are more important than your own.

And then how are you going to ever be truly happy?

Reducing Negativity

Negativity has a huge impact on empaths. They soak it up very quickly. The problem with negative energy is that it is very draining, there is no "up" side to it at all. The best defense is to distance yourself from it as far as possible.

There are no benefits to dealing with negativity – it's not like exercising to get fit and healthy where you persevere and look better in the end. Negative energy can be worked through but there are no real benefits to doing so.

There is so much negativity all around that you never need fear being out of practice in dealing with it.

Do a little experiment this week. Go about your day as you normally would. Read the paper, watch the news, check on your social media, etc. But this time, every time you see something negative, make a small mark in a notebook.

At the end of the week, total all the marks – I am sure that you will be shocked by the results – there is a lot of negativity out there and you encounter it every day.

For the next week, I want you to repeat the exercise but with one major difference – don't check your social media, read the paper or watch TV at all.

At the end of the week, total the results you came up with. I am sure that you will be amazed at how much negativity just this simple exercise cuts out of your life. Think about it for a minute – how much did you miss out on just by not watching the soaps? Do you really want to go back to watching them? Or reading the newspaper?

For the third week, I want you to carry on with the general media ban and take things a step further. How many people do you know that are very negative in nature? We all know to avoid the obvious sad sacks – the people that drone on endlessly about their problems.

But what about those people who seem to be positive but leave you feeling drained after being with them? The ones that offer those stinging backhand compliments?

As far as possible try to exclude negative people from your life. If someone leaves you feeling drained after you have spent time with them, it makes sense to try and exclude them from your life as far as possible.

And, for those instances when that is not possible, minimize your interactions with them and prepare yourself as well as you can upfront. Deal with them when you are feeling strong and confident and this will go a long way to minimizing their negative impact on you.

Chapter 5

Managing Your Own Emotions

Most empaths have trouble dealing with their emotions because they can never be completely sure that the emotions that they are experiencing are their own. It can be painful to deal with emotions and so repressing them may seem like the way to go instead.

In this chapter, we will go through ways in which you can manage your emotions and so lead a healthier and more fulfilled life.

Dealing with Repressed Feelings

Sometimes we have repressed feelings without really even being aware of it. This exercise will help you bring these repressed feelings out in the open so that you can deal with them.

Acknowledge

Start by acknowledging that the feeling is there. We are taught lessons early on in life that make us more prone to repress certain feelings. "Big girls don't cry", "It isn't nice to feel jealous", etc.

Instead of trying to push it under the surface, acknowledge what you are feeling and how it is effecting your body.

Choose to Stay

You have two options now – either to deal with the situation or to run from it. Choose to deal with it, even when the idea of doing so is unpleasant.

Take a few deep breaths and experience the feelings. It is not always going to be fun but it is necessary.

Examine

Take time to examine all aspects of the feeling so that you can visualize it later if you need to. What sensations does your body experience? What other feelings come up as well – perhaps you are feeling anxious and a little excited at the same time.

Scan your body while you are doing this. Visualize the event that led to you feeling this. Where are the sensations the strongest? How strong is the feeling? How threatening is it?

Accept

The physical sensations really don't mean a thing. When this feeing goes away, so will the unpleasant sensations. So, start to actively relax yourself and accept that this will pass as well.

Establish where the heart of the sensation is.

Set Your Intentions

Now that you have an idea of where the sensation is centered and what thought it is linked to, you must now intentionally work to move it out of you. Visualize that thought as a tight ball located inside you and then visualize it moving up and out of your mouth.

Feel the strength of the feeling start to dissipate. Take it in your hand and throw it as far away from you as possible. Feel the relief that this brings.

Breathe

Breathe the new energy and life into your body. Feel the positive energy fill up the space taken up by the physical sensation and feel it radiate out throughout your whole body.

Over time following this exercise will allow you to more easily identify the energy generated by your feelings and the effect that this has on your body.

As you get more comfortable with the process, you will be able to go deeper and deeper into your psyche, eventually working with the self-limiting beliefs buried deep within you. As you continue, you will eventually be able to move through each of these.

Should you come across particularly intense feelings, you can look for some physical outlet for them – like screaming into a pillow or dancing, for example.

This will give you an outlet for those emotions and you will be able to focus your energy more effectively the next time you start to feel an emotion overwhelming you. This exercise is powerful because it neither labels your feelings as good or bad.

All you have to do is to experience them, and feel the full force of them. You don't have to judge whether or not they are correct or "proper". All your feelings are valid because they belong to you. They may not all have a positive effect, but they are all valid.

Releasing Negative Emotions

It is quite natural for empaths to be very emotional and more liable to start crying. Crying is not always a bad thing though – it can help to release the negative feelings. It can be an especially useful outlet when you have feelings that have been repressed for a long time.

If you find that you are battling to release a particular emotion, inducing yourself to cry can be very cathartic. You can do this by watching a movie that is very moving for you or listening to music that will have a similar effect.

Crying is a natural defense mechanism and it helps to give us an outlet for emotions that might otherwise have taken over. It is really a great pity that so many of us are taught from childhood that crying is a weakness when it can be such a help to us.

Using Crowded Areas to Your Advantage

Considering the nature of the empath, this can seem like very contrary advice. However, if you look at things in a different light, you will see that a crowded area can be the ideal testing ground to work on improving your own personal defenses and boundaries.

When you enter an area that has a lot of people in it, visualize your bubble or your light hugging your body tightly and keeping you safe. No negative energy will be able to enter the protective barrier.

Think of it like aversion therapy – you expose yourself to the things that you are afraid of so that you can get used to them and dealing with them. There is nothing like real world practice when it comes to testing your personal shield.

You can practice at home alone all you like but that is not where you are really going to need the help, is it?

If you are nervous about trying the exercise on your own, enlist the aid of a trusted friend or partner on the first few trips. This will help improve your own feelings of security and their positive energy will help to also dispel negative energies in your vicinity.

You probably already know that this is true – haven't you felt that when you go out with someone you trust that you feel less drained on returning? This is because they act as a positive distraction for you.

Enlist the Help of Audio

Another tack to try is to distract yourself with your favorite music or a good audiobook. Just clamp on the earphones and let the sound drown out all the noises around you.

This, in combination with the energy barrier that you have visualized can be extremely effective at protecting you from negative emotions.

It is also extremely effective if there is something in particular that you want to work on. The audio focuses your attention.

It is also an effective way of removing yourself from the general stream of energy around you – you alone can hear what is being played on the earphones and this, in itself, gives a level of separation for you.

Chapter 6

Keep Yourself Clear of Psychic Baggage

Empaths are naturally drawn to helping and healing other people. If you are an empath, you are no doubt happiest being able to help others. It is the empath's best trait but also their worst failing.

With the focus being on healing others, most empaths neglect the person that is most important in their lives – themselves. This quickly leads to burnout and a reduced efficiency when it comes to healing.

In order to be an effective empath, you need to ensure that you are healed completely yourself. The good news is that, as an empath, healing comes naturally to you – even when that means healing yourself.

The limit of your powers depends on how much confidence you have in yourself, what your intentions are, what you believe, and how able you are to live with love and compassion.

Living with love and compassion becomes extremely difficult when we have serious emotional wounds. Most of the empath's wounds stem from fear. Whether it is a fear that they will be hurt, a fear that they are not good enough or a fear that they cannot trust in themselves or others.

Most empaths would have been wounded by someone that they cared deeply for or admired. Think about it for a few minutes yourself – what was the most serious emotional wound that you sustained? Can you remember what it was that first made you fearful?

If we can pin down what caused the initial emotional wound, that is wonderful because it gives you a starting point. If you cannot pin down something in particular, you will need to work by instinct – you will instinctively know when you are headed on the right path and when you are not.

For most empaths, improving their self-esteem may be problematic. This is especially the case because they often believe that they need to put the needs of others ahead of the needs of themselves.

They often find that their compassion and willingness to help are seen as a weakness and they might find themselves being exploited as a result.

And, unfortunately, this willingness to help others leads them to want to help those who are not always deserving of it. They might come across personality types that want to take full advantage of their natures and suck out as much energy as possible. Empaths are of particular interest to narcissists. And a relationship with a narcissist is the last thing any empath needs because it is particularly damaging to them.

The empath is also particularly attractive to energy vampires who will take full advantage of the situation without giving anything in return.

Another problem that empaths may encounter is that they tend to be disregarded as too emotional.

The empath puts up with all this because they do not yet understand that they are just as deserving of a healthy relationship as everyone else. They do not properly understand that they are not responsible for the happiness of others and that they do not need to take responsibility for fixing others.

What the empath needs to come to realize is that everyone is responsible for their own happiness. While some people can be supported, they also need to make the effort to improve their own lives.

The empath also needs to get some support out of the relationship – healthy relationships are about give and take.

Returning Energy

This exercise is about returning the negative energy that has been sent to you by others. Start off by acknowledging any feelings or hurt or pain that you may be experiencing as a result of this.

Understand that this is not a blame game. You should try to reserve judgement on the other person as this can prevent you from moving on from the encounter.

You also need to realize that carrying this person's negative energy or pain is not actually helping them at all. They will only truly heal when they work through these emotions themselves.

In fact, by taking on these feelings for them, you are actually getting in the way of their healing. By letting them avoid dealing with the emotions, you are also preventing them from moving forward from them.

Your next step is to return the feelings to them. Visualize the feelings that you have identified as theirs, in much the same way as you visualized the negative feelings taking the shape of a ball in the earlier exercise.

Now visualize those feelings all congregating in a single space and see yourself actually draining that space. Visualize the feelings moving out from you and back to their real owner. Choose whatever form you like as long as you can visualize the feelings going back to them.

Repeat this exercise until you are positive that it has worked thoroughly.

Psychic Attacks and Energy Vampires

There are a lot of different types of people that the empath must defend themselves against but the energy vampire is the one that is most likely to be encountered. These are very damaged individuals who are emotionally stunted and who believe that everything is centered on them.

For the most part, they are not able to see things from someone else's point of view. They are polar opposites to the empath in that they usually have little or no empathy.

Narcissists are also energy vampires but they go one step further in that they believe that everyone exists to serve their purposes. The energy vampire will soak up as much energy from the empath as possible.

The narcissist, on the other hand, will actively work at creating a situation where the empath is completely reliant on them. They will ensure that the empath is always off-balance and seek to put the empath in situations that are unpleasant for them. The narcissist thrives on the misery of others and keeping them off balance.

In most cases, the energy vampires and narcissists have no idea that there is anything wrong with them. Dealing with them is very draining. Spend too much time in their company and you risk damaging your psyche.

It can be difficult for the empath to defend themselves against these personality types because these people are so overbearing. They are constantly looking for ways to gain the upper hand and to gather more energy and this makes them very dangerous to the empath.

If you spend too much time with them, you will start to feel negative and completely and utterly spent. If you find that you feel very downtrodden or depressed after every interaction with a specific person, it is likely that they are an energy vampire and that they should be completely avoided.

Why are These People Like This?

These people are actually pitiable in that they have very deep feelings of being unlovable or that they are not worth loving. This is what prevents them from meeting their own emotional needs. They are less able to feel emotions and generate their own positive psychic energy.

As a result, they have to get the energy from others. They are pitiable in that they truly need help but there is no way to actually help them. They will generally be unaware of there being anything wrong with the way they behave and will hardly ever see that they need to change.

They may even come across as evil but this is not strictly fair. They really do not understand that what they are doing is wrong and they will always have a justification for their actions in their own minds. This justification will generally sound ridiculous to "normal" people but it makes perfect sense to them.

In a way, they are also victims. Something in their lives has convinced them that they are deeply unworthy of love and made them incapable of feeling it. They are very much attracted to the empath because the empath desperately wants to help them.

They find it easy to prey on empaths because the empath is so open to them. Normally speaking, they will keep the attachment going until they find a new target or tire of the game.

At the end of the day, it is best to run if you come across this personality type. They will end up convincing you that anything that is wrong is your fault and they will suck out all your energy. You are not capable of saving them, no matter how much you want to. They are going to drag you down so cut off ties with them as quickly as you can.

As with all things in life, there are differing degrees when it comes to energy vampires. Maybe it only shows itself when they are having a bad time. Analyze your friendships. If they call on you when they are having a bad time, it is normal to let them talk it out. However, it's important that you consciously detach from the situation so that you don't take on their negativity.

Also consider how much of a two-way street the relationship is. Are you the one who does all the listening? Do they support you when you need it as well? A healthy relationship means that there is a balance between giving and taking support. You cannot have one person doing all the taking and the other doing all the giving.

If you find yourself in a relationship where you do all the giving, you need to either find a way to change it so it is more balanced, or you need to cut them loose.

Energetic Cording

The most effective way to stop this malicious influence is to stop interacting with the person altogether. Wish them well and then just stop visiting them or taking their calls.

But what do you do when it is someone that you work with or a family member and it is not possible to cut them out of your life?

This is where cording comes in. Cording relates to the energetic connection that exists between people.

People who have a relationship of some sort will have an energetic cord that exists between them.

When this is a healthy relationship, energy will flow both ways and both people will feel uplifted when in each other's presence. In a healthy relationship, the formation of this cord occurs naturally.

But it can also be a forced connection. If someone wants to drain your energy, they can force the connection. In this case, the energy only flows from you to them. They will feel uplifted by the connection but you will not. You will leave encounters with them feeling drained.

It is in such cases that the cord needs to be broken. If you do not do this, you can still lose vital energy to that person, even when they are not in close proximity. This can manifest in you not being able to stop thinking about them, for example. This is normally an indication that they are thinking about you as well.

The problem is that the physical distance between the two of you is not enough to prevent this cord from being attached.

When you start to heal and work on your boundaries and defenses, however, you can break these cords.

Energetic cording is most common in the chakras of the solar plexus, sacral, throat or heart. Aches that seem to appear there for no good reason may be an indication that energetic cording has occurred.

You can help to break the connection by physically protecting one of these chakras – that is the reason we instinctively cross our arms when we are in an uncomfortable social situation.

You can also wear crystals over the relevant chakras to help defend the energy. Stones such as lapis lazuli, tiger's eye, etc. are powerful protection against unwanted energetic cording.

It is easier to defend yourself if your chakras are clear and in good working order. You should practice a chakra clearing meditation at least once a week to ensure that they are healthy. You can use crystals placed over each of the relevant chakras to help you balance them again.

The solar plexus chakra is the most vulnerable as this is where our emotions are seated. This is often the chakra that is most susceptible to emotional damage and one that can be exploited by energy vampires.

An unbalanced solar plexus chakra can manifest in digestive problems and problems with your stomach. If you are finding that you constantly have problems in this region, it is a good idea to rebalance the solar plexus chakra.

Cutting the Cord

There will be instances when you need to cut these cords in order to maintain your own equilibrium and health. This is especially true when you have been involved in a particularly toxic and damaging relationship.

These cords do not simply dissolve once they have been established and so you need to consciously carry out this exercise in order to break them.

If you are unsure of whether or not the person is connected to you by an energetic cord but you feel that the relationship is detrimental to you, it is a good idea to complete this exercise. Even if there is no actual cord in place, this exercise helps to set the intention that you want to break from them energetically and it can help to safeguard your energy.

Go somewhere that you won't be interrupted, sit calmly and relax completely. Take a few deep breaths in and out to aid in relaxation.

Now visualize the other person standing directly in front of you. Can you see which chakra the cord is attached to? (It could be in the form or pure energy, or a more practical visualization such as a rope or a piece of tubing.)

If you cannot visualize the cord straight away, don't be concerned – these connections are not always easy to spot. Visualize a cord connecting one of your chakras to one of their chakras.

Request that your energy be returned to you and that their energy be returned to them. You can visualize the energy moving along the cord.

Now visualize you actually cutting the length of cord with a pair of scissors or a knife. Cut it as close to your chakra as you are able.

Now you can ask what caused you to attract this particular experience. Were you holding on to some negative belief? While it is tempting to believe that we are a victim when it comes to the bad things that happen in our life, the truth is that these are specific circumstances that we learn from. They are probably life lessons that we chose to learn before we incarnated into this life.

By ignoring this, we are not learning the lesson and are bound to make the same mistake over and over again.

Close off the exercise by sending love and compassion to the party that injured you. Actively practice forgiving them and realize that they were doing the best they could with the level of knowledge that they had. Let them go in light.

Conclusion

Well here we are. Well done for getting through the whole book.

If you are an empath, I hope that this book has helped you in creating real life changes that make it easier to cope. If you are not an empath, but know someone who is, I hope that this book has given you more insight into the world of an empath.

Empaths are incredibly important light workers and do a lot of good work. At the end of the day though, they also need to ensure that they do look after themselves. Being in the best shape physically and emotionally makes it possible for you to reach your true potential as an empath and makes it possible for you to help more people.

One of the hardest lessons that an empath has to learn, though, is that they cannot help everyone. I hope that this book has taught you that there is a distinction between those that can be helped and those that cannot. I hope that you are able to more easily make the distinction yourself now.

Being an empath can be tough at times but it is also incredibly rewarding. I hope that this book has highlighted the importance of this gift for you.

I wish you light and love on your healing journey.

A message from the author, Jane Aniston

To show my appreciation for your support, Id like to offer you a couple of exclusive free gifts:

FREE BONUS!

As a free bonus, I've included a preview of one of my other best-selling books directly after this section. Enjoy!

FREE BONUS!: Preview Of

"Narcissist - How To Beat The Narcissist! Understanding Narcissism & Narcissistic Personality Disorder"

If you enjoyed this book, I have a little bonus for you; a preview of one of my other books, "Narcissist - How To Beat The Narcissist! Understanding Narcissism & Narcissistic Personality Disorder". Enjoy!

Introduction

Narcissism is a hot topic nowadays. Some people say that society is becoming more and more narcissistic. Is the present preoccupation with selfies proof of our increasing narcissism and is the Internet to blame? Is narcissism always a bad thing? Can a narcissist be a productive and valued member of society? Are all narcissists dangerous and heartless? What causes narcissism?

Although we know that a narcissist is a person who has an inflated sense of self, there are many things we need to learn about narcissism. Who is a narcissist? How can you tell if a person is a narcissist? Why do people get trapped in relationships with narcissists and how can they get away? Is a narcissist the same as a person with Narcissistic Personality Disorder (NPD)?

There is so much to know about narcissism. This book will try to explain things in simple terms. If you don't want to sift through all the medical jargon and you just want to understand narcissism in plain English, this is for you.

Why is it important to understand narcissism? You may be in a relationship with a narcissist and not know it. Knowing how to spot one and what to do about it can relieve you of much anguish.

Understanding narcissism will help prevent you from falling into the narcissist's trap and help you to cope with the narcissists you have to deal with. Learning to deal with narcissists can empower you. This book hopes to help you break free if you are in the narcissist's hold and find strength in yourself.

Chapter 1

Narcissus and Echo

It's interesting how seemingly innocent children's stories, fairytales or fables can speak universal truths and help us understand complex psychological conditions. Greek mythology has always been interesting and entertaining to many and the story of Narcissus is a fascinating tale from which narcissism got its name. There are many versions of this story but let me tell it to you as I remember it.

It's a story of a handsome young youth by the name of Narcissus. When Narcissus was born, his mother brought him to the blind prophet Tiresias and asked if her son would live long. Tiresias replied: "He'll have a long life as long as he never knows himself."

When Narcissus grew older, his good looks attracted many- mortal and immortal alike. Nymphs and fairies followed him everywhere he went, trying to win his heart and attention. But Narcissus paid no attention to them and simply went about his hunting duties.

Among the wood nymphs and fairies who were crazy about Narcissus was Echo. Echo was a very talkative wood nymph and this somehow didn't sit well with the goddess Hera. Hera was so piqued, it seemed, with Echo's long-windedness, that she placed a curse on the hapless wood-nymph. Poor Echo would no longer be able to say what was on her mind but was doomed to simply repeat whatever was spoken to her. So, Echo could not express her love for the very fetching and charming Narcissus. She continued to stalk him, however, and believed she could still find a way to let him know of her undying love for him.

It is said that, once, Narcissus sensed he was being followed and called out to whoever was there. Of course, Echo could only repeat his words. When he did see her, he was unimpressed and even somewhat repulsed. Echo was clearly beautiful and beguiling but she didn't seem to be his type. She continued to pursue him, however, waiting for the right moment to finally let him know how she felt for him.

Remember, it wasn't only Echo who was smitten by Narcissus. Many others were infatuated with his good looks, but Narcissus rejected them all. Narcissus seemed incapable of falling in love at that time. This soon came to the ears of Nemesis, the goddess of divine retribution. Some call her the goddess of vengeance. A rejected lover had purportedly asked Nemesis to never let Narcissus be loved in return.

In one of his hunting trips, Narcissus gets thirsty and looks around for a place to get a drink. He comes upon a pond and crouches down to drink water. This is the moment that Narcissus glimpses his reflection in the mirror-clear water and promptly falls in love with himself. Some people say the water was enchanted and that it had cast its spell on Narcissus, making him unable to get away.

Narcissus is completely unaware that he has fallen madly in love with his own image in the water. He tries to speak to it, to ask questions. At this point, Echo, who is still lurking about, thinks she has found the opportunity to tell him her feelings. Whenever

Narcissus says "I love you" to his reflection, Echo repeats it back to him. But Narcissus is still oblivious to Echo and is hopelessly enamored with his reflection. He tries hard to get some kind of response from his reflection and refuses to leave the side of the pond. There he stays, simply gazing at himself, perhaps hoping to get some kind of requital from his image; fantasizing until he eventually weakens and dies. Others say he tries to reach for his reflection and drowns in the pond; others say he committed suicide.

Soon after, where Narcissus once crouched gazing at himself, the plant named after him first sprung up, with beautiful flowers gazing down at the water. Echo, on the other hand, still pined for him even though he was already gone. She soon wasted away, fading until only her voice remained in the mountains.

This story is filled with insights on self-love and how it affects people around you. Echo is sometimes forgotten when this story is retold, but the significance of her role in the narcissist's web should not be overlooked.

Clearly, Narcissus turned away everyone who tried to have some degree of intimacy with him. He rejected them because they loved him, and he was incapable of love at that time. When he did fall in love, it was with an image – an illusion. And, it was with himself. Similarly, the person who tries to establish a relationship with the narcissist may only be able to do so if he or she is willing to simply reflect the narcissist's own views. If you want to get the narcissist attention, you must simply echo his ideas and opinions, you must be in total agreement with him. Just like Echo, your voice or opinion may be reduced simply to a repetition of the narcissist's. And your identity will be reduced to a mist, a whisper devoid of body or personality.

The narcissist is unaware of how much he adores himself and he is most likely unaware of how he can ruin lives. He may be aware but he doesn't care. Like Narcissus in the story, he may not know his true self. He may only know or see the image he has built of himself.

It is also interesting to note how Echo desperately continues to long for Narcissus' attention, despite his disagreeable attitude and behavior. She continues to declare her love for him and wait for him in spite of everything. What's more, it's strange that she would be so smitten by someone only because of his looks. In the end she is reduced to a hardly discernible whisper. Such may be the fate of one who offers all of his or her loyalty and adulation to the narcissist.

Check out the rest of "Narcissist - How To Beat The Narcissist! Understanding Narcissism & Narcissistic Personality Disorder" on the Amazon store!

Check Out My Other Books!

Understanding Anxiety - *Why You're Suffering From Anxiety & How You Can Start Breaking Free!*

Overcoming Anxiety *-Practical Approaches You Can Use To Manage Fear & Anxiety In The Moment & Long Term*

Depression - Practical & Natural Approaches You Can Use To Cure Depression In The Moment & Long Term

Cognitive Behavioral Therapy - A Practical Guide To C.B.T. For Overcoming Anxiety, Depression, Addictions & Other Psychological Conditions

Homemade Shampoo (Includes 34 Organic Shampoo Recipes!)

Homemade Makeup (Includes 28 Organic Makeup Recipes!)

Homemade Deodorant (Includes 20 Organic Deodorant Recipes!)

Homemade Lip Balm (Includes 22 Organic Lip Balm Recipes!)

Homemade Bath Salts (Includes 35 Organic Bath Salt Recipes!)

All books available as ebooks or printed books

Printed in Great Britain
by Amazon